Rain

by Grace Hansen

abdopublishing.com

Published by Abdo Kids, a division of ABDO, PO Box 398166, Minneapolis, Minnesota 55439.

Printed in the United States of America, North Mankato, Minnesota.

052015

092015

 THIS BOOK CONTAINS
RECYCLED MATERIALS

Photo Credits: iStock

Production Contributors: Teddy Borth, Jennie Forsberg, Grace Hansen

Design Contributors: Laura Rask, Dorothy Toth

Library of Congress Control Number: 2014958417

Cataloging-in-Publication Data

Hansen, Grace.

Rain / Grace Hansen.

p. cm. -- (Weather)

ISBN 978-1-62970-932-1

Includes index.

1. Rain--Juvenile literature.   I. Title.

551--dc23

2014958417

Table of Contents

Evaporation

The sun heats bodies of water. Heat makes water turn into **vapor**. Vapor goes into the air. This is called **evaporation**.

5

Warm air rises. It takes the **vapor** with it. Warm air rises when cold air blows in. Mountains can also make warm air rise.

7

Condensation

Warm air cools as it rises. **Vapor** turns to tiny droplets in cold air. The droplets come together. They form a cloud. This is called **condensation**.

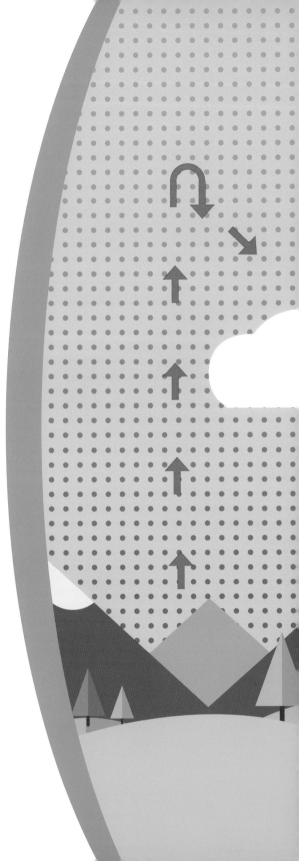

Precipitation

Water droplets come together in big clouds. The water droplets get bigger. They fall from the clouds when they get too heavy.

When water falls from clouds it is raining. Rain is also called **precipitation**.

13

Too Much, Too Little, and Just Right

Too much rain is a bad thing. The ground can become too wet. Trees can fall over. It can also cause flooding.

Not enough rain is also a bad thing. This can cause a **drought**. All living things need water to live.

Rain is an important part of the water cycle. Rain brings fresh water to plants and animals.

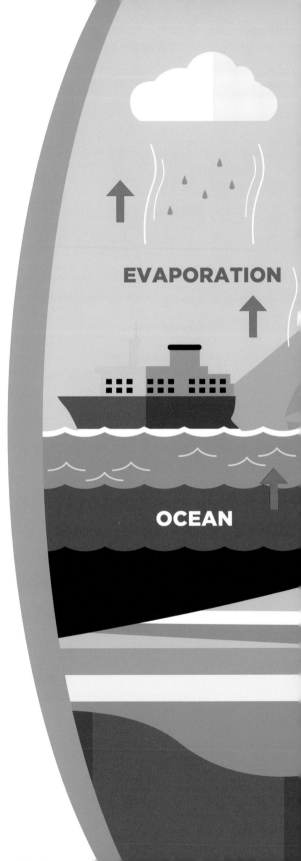

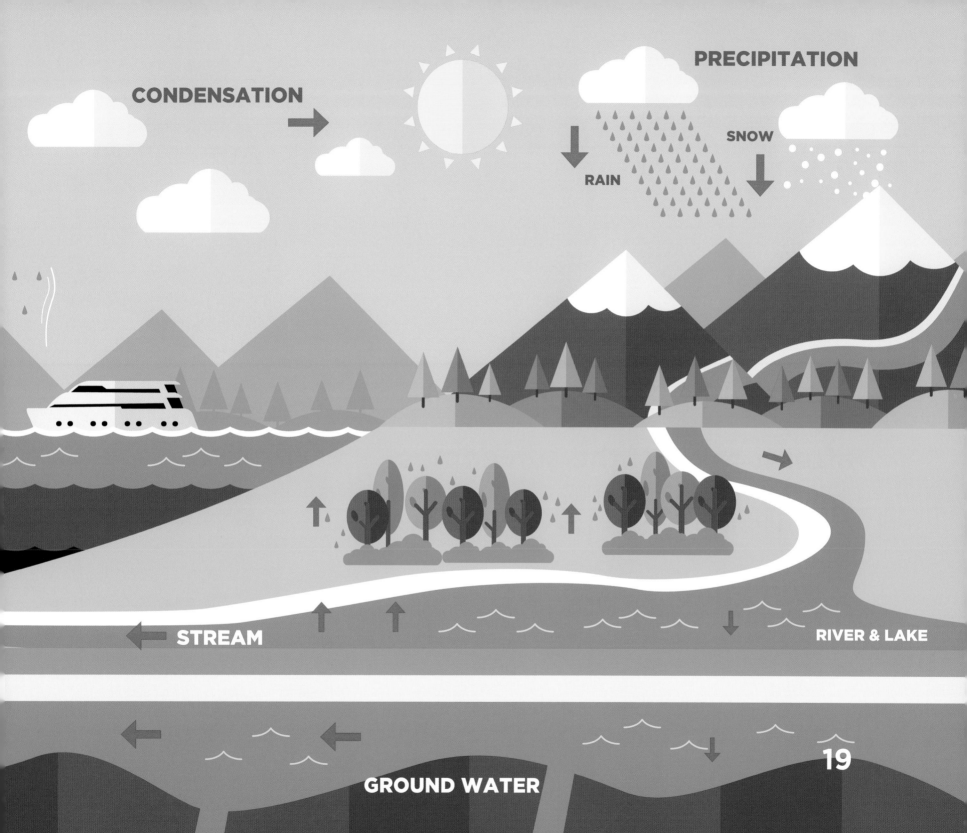

After the Rain

Water droplets are in the air after it rains. If the sun comes out, its light hits the droplets. And a rainbow appears!

The Water Cycle

Condensation

Precipitation

Evaporation

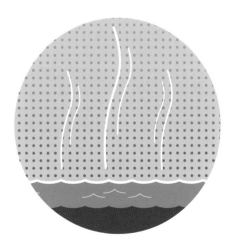

22

Glossary

condensation – the process of condensing. Condensing is to change to a denser form, like from a gas to a solid or a liquid.

drought – a long period of time with very little rainfall. It damages plants and crops.

evaporation – the process of evaporating. Evaporating is to change from a liquid or solid state into vapor.

precipitation – rain, snow, sleet, etc., formed by condensation.

vapor – the gas form of a liquid. Water vapor is the gas form of water. It is made from evaporation.

23

Index

abdokids.com

Use this code to log on to abdokids.com and access crafts, games, videos, and more!

Abdo Kids Code:
WRK9321